The Advanced Guitar Case Chord Book

by Askold Buk

**Carry it everywhere. Clear, readable diagrams.
Fits into your guitar case. Examples of every type of chord.**

GW00642960

Cover photography by Luciano Viti/Retna Ltd.
Interior design and layout by Len Vogler

Order No. AM 80227
US International Standard Book Number: 0.8256.1243.8
UK International Standard Book Number: 0.7119.2334.5

Exclusive Distributors:
Music Sales Corporation
257 Park Avenue South, New York, NY 10010 USA
Music Sales Limited
8/9 Frith Street, London W1V 5TZ England
Music Sales Pty. Limited
120 Rothschild Street, Rosebery, Sydney, NSW 2018, Australia

Printed in the United States of America by
Vicks Lithograph and Printing Corporation

Amsco Publications
New York/London/Sydney

Contents

Introduction

If you have ever gotten stuck on a chord when playing from a songbook, or wondered how your favorite guitarists played those "magic" chords you couldn't figure out, then this book is for you.

Like most guitarists, you have probably become frustrated with the chord diagrams provided in most pop sheet music and songbooks. These arrangements are usually done by keyboard players, with stock guitar chord diagrams added as an afterthought. Even in more thoughtfully arranged sheet music, the chords will usually be given in somewhat simplified forms so as to be accessible to guitarists of limited experience. The assumption is that a more seasoned guitarist will want to create a more personal arrangement by substituting more authentic or tasteful voicings of the basic chords provided. But even if you look in a chord dictionary, how do you know which voicing is the right one? And how come so many of them sound so bad?

You see, in order to play the correct voicings, you have to really hear them in the context of the progression or song. This book allows you to do just that. Not only are the most popular voicings (used by professional guitarists of all styles) given, but each chord group comes with at least one practical example included, so you can instantaneously apply not only your fingers, but also your ears. Every genre of music is covered, from jazz to heavy metal, from Miles Davis to Whitney Houston to Van Halen. You'll learn by doing, and you'll never be stuck searching for that lost chord again.

How to Use This Book

Most people assume that there are rock chords which are different from jazz chords, which in turn are different from country chords, and so on. This is not true: It's the way in which various voicings are applied that counts. For example, in this book you'll find the same chords used in a Frank Sinatra song as in a Living Colour song.

To get the most out of this book, you should know the open position chords (Major, Minor, and Dominant Seventh), and some common bar chords. You should also know some common progressions (I-IV-V; I-VIm-IIm-V; etc.).

In order to assimilate a new chord, you must able to hear it first. Go through a chord group and pick out the voicings you're most comfortable with. Play the example(s) given with the particular chord group, and hear how the new chord works within a typical progression. Try to relate the new sound to a familiar one—something you are used to playing. Experiment using the different voicings in the chord group with the example. Make a note of which ones work and which ones don't.

Notice that the individual voices (R, 3, 5, 7, etc.) are shown in each chord diagram. This will help you with your own voicings. (Refer to the substitution principles in the following section.) Experiment with changing a Dominant Seventh chord to a Seventh Flat-Nine or Augmented Seventh Sharp-Nine. See which tones fall where on the neck.

On the small chance that you run across a chord that you don't see in this book, reduce it to a simpler voicing (make sure you keep the third and seventh). For example, if you see G13♭5♭9, you may play G13♭9, G13, or even G7. Conversely, you can take a basic voicing and try extending or altering the chord. For example, if you see a G7 chord, try playing G9, G13, or even G13♯11. Let your ear be the final judge.

Keep these pointers in mind:

- Be aware of the melody note (the top note of the chord). Usually an extended chord will have the alteration in the top voice.

- Don't put the altered/extended notes in the bass (as the lowest note). This will blur the harmonic function of the chord.

- Try to achieve smooth voice-leading when putting together your own progressions. Avoid wide jumps in the harmony. Try to voice-lead with half-step and whole-step motion. Play through some of the IIm-V-I progressions in the book, then come up with your own.

- Keep experimenting. Some of the greatest innovations in harmony were a result of an inquisitive mind combined with trial-and-error.

Play what you love. Love what you play. Good Luck!

Basic Theory

Generally speaking, there are three tonal qualities in Western music: major, minor, and dominant. Any chord will fit into one of these categories. Major chords are generally described as "happy"; minor as "sad"; and dominant as "tense," "leading," or "needing to be resolved." The tones that determine whether the chord is major, minor, or dominant are the third and the seventh. Major chords always contain the third and the seventh. Minor chords always have the flatted third. Dominant chords always have the third and the flatted seventh.

The nature of the guitar's tuning often limits playing complete voicings of five- or six-note chords. Therefore, you have to substitute extended and altered chord tones for nonessential ones. Since the only truly essential tones are the third and the seventh, you may freely replace the other tones without changing the nature of the chord. Here is a substitution chart for reference.

9, ♭9, or ♯9	*replaces*	Root
sus2 or sus4	*replaces*	3*
♭5, ♯5, ♯11, or 13	*replaces*	5

---

* These tones usually resolve to the third. When left unresolved, they produce an ambiguous (neither major nor minor) sound that is useful in many types of modern music.

Major Chords

Cmaj7

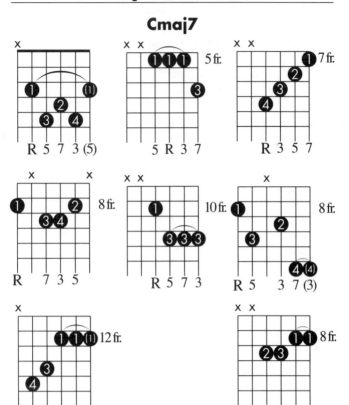

C6

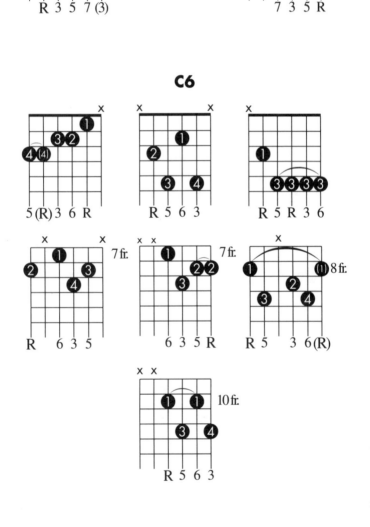

Major Seventh chords sound fuller than simple major triads. Listen to the Beatles' "Here, There, and Everywhere" or the Cure's "Boys Don't Cry," and then play this example.

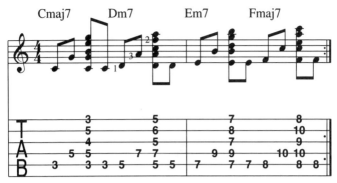

Major Seventh chords are widely used in rhythm and blues music. Here is a riff similar to the one in "I'll Be Around" by the Spinners.

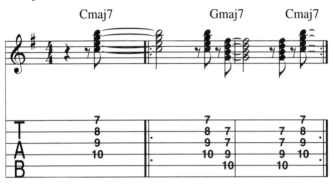

The Major Sixth chord is *the* classic ending chord found in a lot of early Beatles songs. Here is an example.

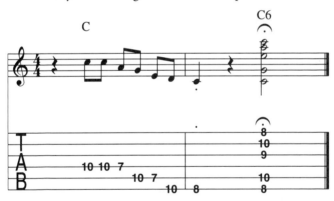

This example is a common progression used in pop music. Listen to "After the Lovin'" by Engelbert Humperdink or "Can't Smile" by Barry Manilow. Notice that though only one voice in the C chord changes (C to B to A to B), the result is rather effective.

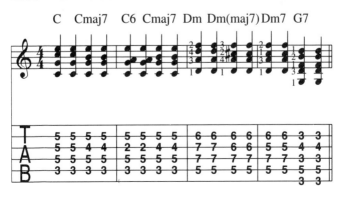

Csus4

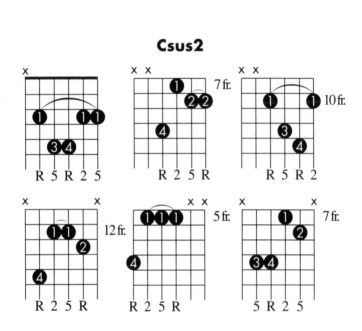

Csus2

C^{sus2}_{sus4}

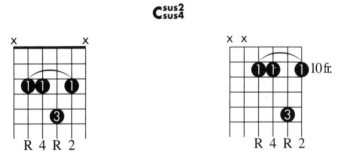

Listen to Led Zeppelin's "Kashmir" for a great example of Suspended Fourth chords.

"Hold Your Head Up" by Argent is another great suspended-chord workout.

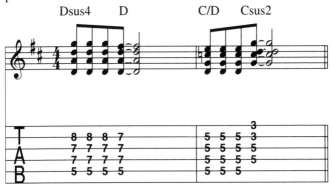

Arpeggiating Suspended Second chords produces an open, airy sound. Listen to the introduction to "Every Little Thing She Does Is Magic" by the Police.

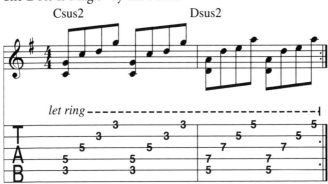

In folk music, suspended chords are used to break up static chord vamps, such as the one in "Tangled Up in Blue" by Bob Dylan.

Cmaj9

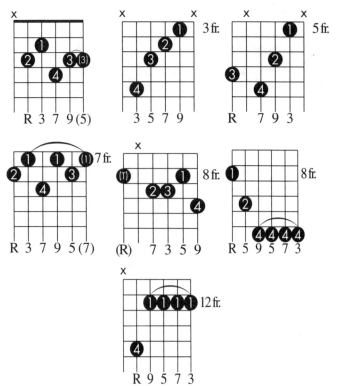

C⁶/9

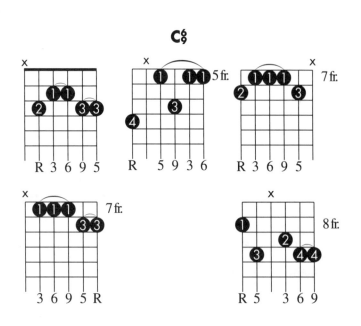

The Major Ninth chord is commonly used in jazz. It is a very "big-sounding" chord. You might want to use it in the verse to "Somewhere over the Rainbow."

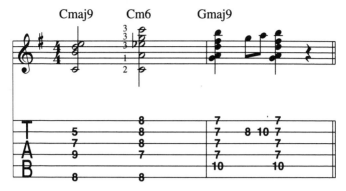

In contemporary rhythm and blues music, Major Ninth chords are often used as substitutes for major triads. "Sweet Love" by Anita Baker is a good example.

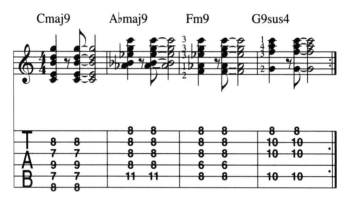

The Six-Nine chord is a sound favored by country western and rockabilly musicians. Here is a classic ending lick.

Here are the first three bars to the jazz standard "All of Me" arranged in chord-melody style. Notice the various types of C major chords used as substitutions for the original C triad.

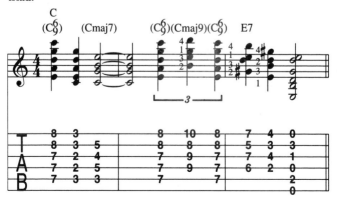

13

C6♯11 (C6♭5)

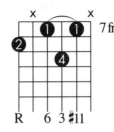
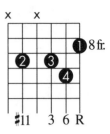

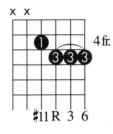

Cmaj7♯11 (Cmaj7♭5)

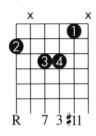
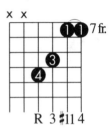

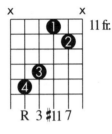

Cmaj9♯11 (Cmaj9♭5)

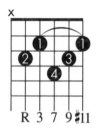
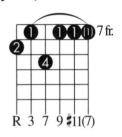

Cmaj13♯11 (Cmaj13♭5)

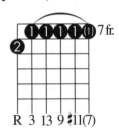

The pop classic "That's What Friends Are For" employs the Major Sixth Flat-Five chord. Here is a similar progression. (As the more theoretically minded among you will no doubt have noticed, you could also think of the C6♭5 chord in this example as an F#m7♭5.)

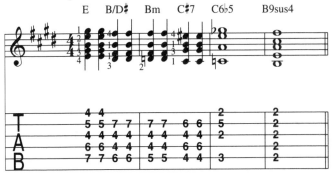

There are two applications for the Major Seventh Sharp-Eleven chord: as a dramatic ending chord or as the IV chord in songs such as "Moon River" or "Someday My Prince Will Come."

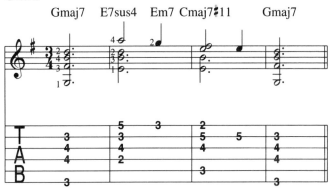

Probably the most common progression in Western music is the IIm-V-I. Here is an example using sharp-eleven chords. Notice that the D♭9#11 is used as a substitute for G7.

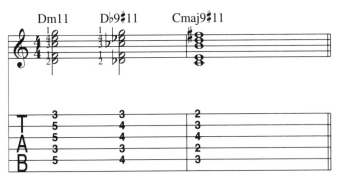

This example resembles the Philadelphia-rock/white-soul sound, as popularized by Hall and Oates, or "Hideaway" by Todd Rundgren.

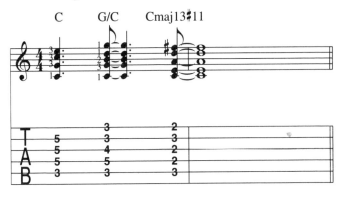

Cmaj13

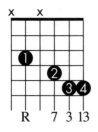

R   7 3 13

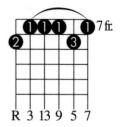

R 3 13 9 5 7

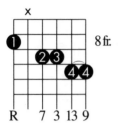

R   7 3 13 9

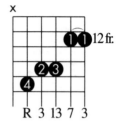

R 3 13 7 3

Here is another IIm-V-I progression. The flat-five substitution principle (D♭7♯9 for G7) is used here again.

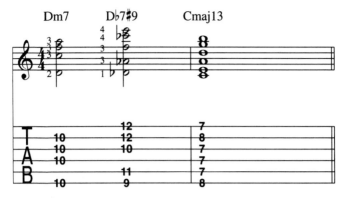

Minor Chords

Dm7

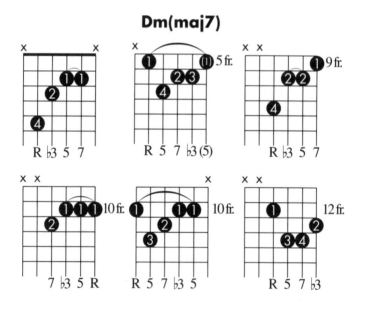

Dm(maj7)

Here is a funky way to use the Minor Seventh chord. Listen to "Long Train Runnin'" by the Doobie Brothers.

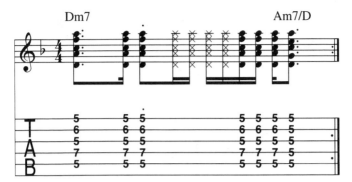

This progression is similar to the introduction to "Billie Jean" by Michael Jackson.

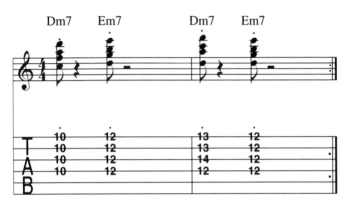

The Minor (Major Seven) chord is a dark, moody sound favored by television and film composers. Here is an idea that resembles "Harlem Nocturne" (the theme from *Mike Hammer*).

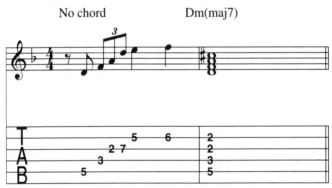

Here is another application of this chord. The root of a minor triad descends chromatically to the sixth. This move is commonly used in Latin music, such as Sade's "Smooth Operator."

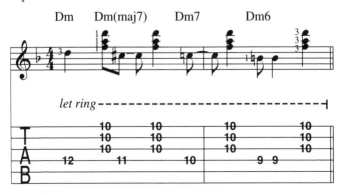

Dm6

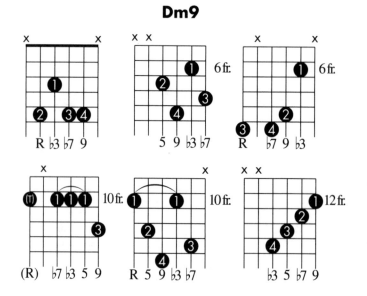

Dm9

The IV to IVm to I progression can be found in songs ranging from the Beatles ("If I Fell") to Extreme ("More than Words"). Play this progression.

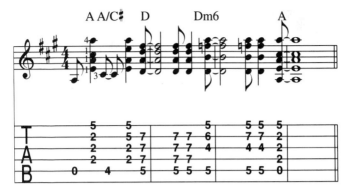

The Minor Sixth chord is widely used in funk music. Here is a funky riff that Prince might play.

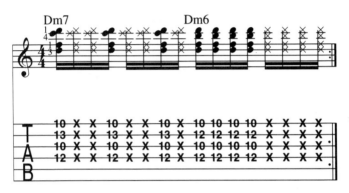

Here is a common progression resembling "Lowdown" by Boz Scaggs or "Spooky" by the Classics IV.

The Minor Ninth chord is showcased in the first bar of the standard "When Sunny Gets Blue." Play this chord-melody idea.

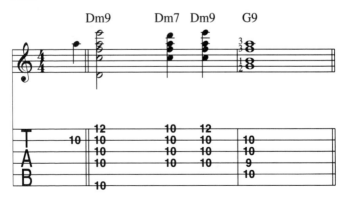

Dm⁶/₉

R ♭3 6 9

♭3 6 9 5

8 fr.
♭3 6 9 5 R

R ♭3 6 9 — 10 fr.

Dm9 (maj7)

R ♭3 7 9

5 fr.
♭3 5 7 9

6 fr.
5 9 ♭3 7

10 fr.
7 ♭3 5 9

Dm11

R ♭3 ♭7 9 11

5 fr.
R 11 ♭7 ♭3 5

8 fr.
R ♭7 ♭3 11

Dm11

12 fr.
(5) R 11 ♭7 ♭3

Dm 13

3 fr.
R ♭3 ♭7 9 13

Dm 13

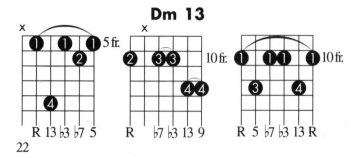

5 fr.
R 13 ♭3 ♭7 5

10 fr.
R ♭7 ♭3 13 9

10 fr.
R 5 ♭7 ♭3 13 R

22

This orchestral study is reminiscent of the theme from the television show *Perry Mason.* Notice the powerful sound of the first chord.

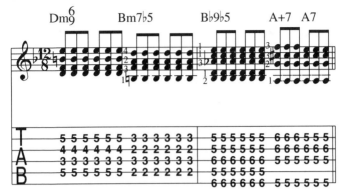

Here is a progression inspired by the classic "Stairway to Heaven." It is a great study in counterpoint.

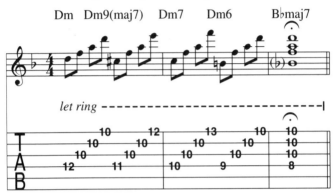

The Minor Eleventh chord works great in funk music. Here is an Ohio Players kind of groove.

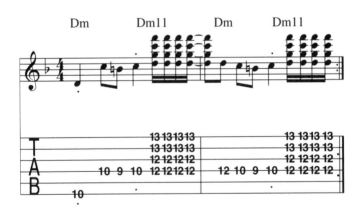

This bombastic progression was used in the fifties classic "Boulevard of Broken Dreams." Reduced, it is simply Dm to A7.

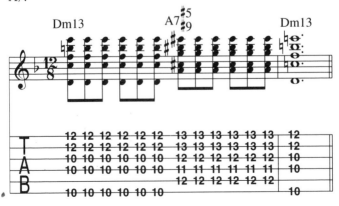

Dm7♭5

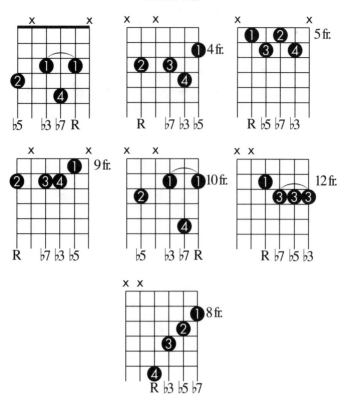

Dm7♯5

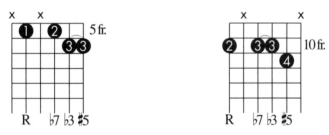

The Minor Seventh Flat-Five chord is usually used as the IIm chord in a minor key. Here is vamp that can be used in "Blue Bossa."

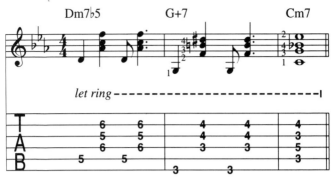

This idea sounds like the lift to the chorus of "She's Come Undone" by the Guess Who.

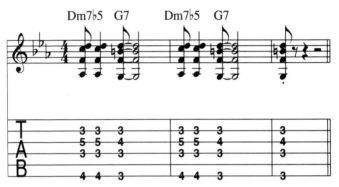

The Minor Seventh Sharp-Five chord is favored by fusion artists such as Larry Carlton. Listen to "Room 335."

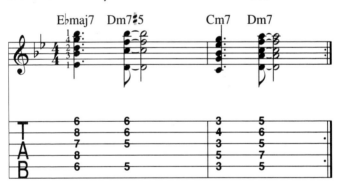

This chord is often used as the IIIm chord in the harmonized major scale. Here is a typical gospel and rhythm and blues turnaround such as you can hear in Barbara Mason's "Yes, I'm Ready."

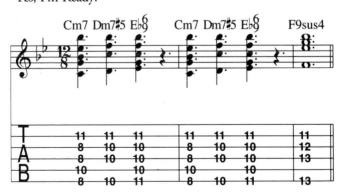

Dominant Chords

G7

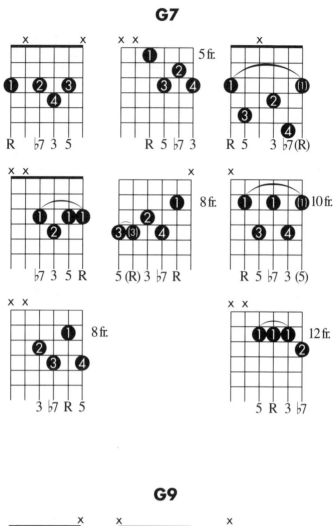

G9

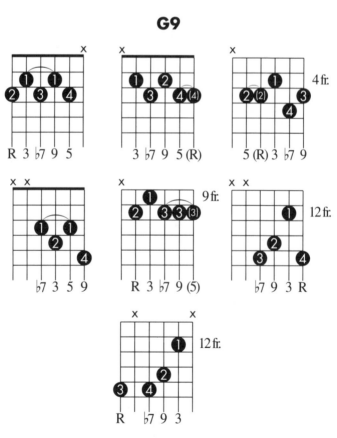

Here is a classic blues introduction. Listen to "Red House" by Jimi Hendrix, and play this example.

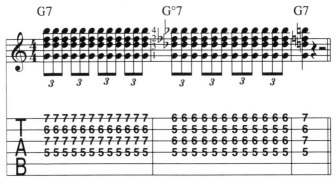

The Seventh chord is primarily used as the V7 in a progression. It wants to resolve to the I chord, as in this study, reminiscent of the Beatles' "Twist and Shout."

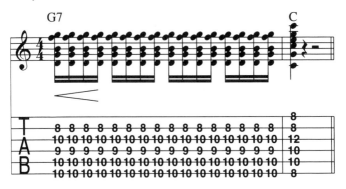

"The Rain Song" by Led Zeppelin uses this voicing of a Ninth chord. Here's a similar idea.

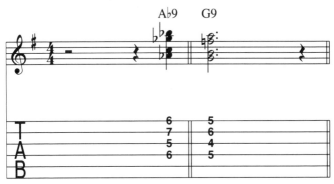

This is the classic Ninth-chord sound made popular by James Brown and scores of funk artists. Listen to "I Feel Good."

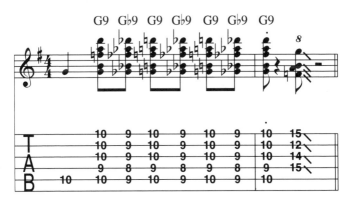

G7sus4

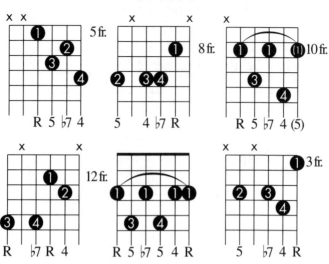

G7b5

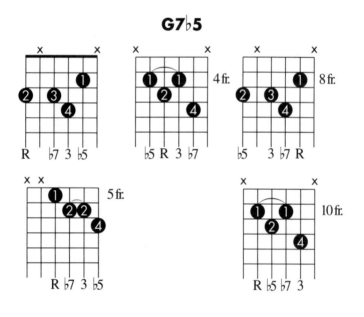

This chord is a part of the history of rock and roll. Listen to the first big chord in "A Hard Day's Night" by the Beatles.

The Eurythmics used a similar arpeggiated figure in their introduction to "Would I Lie to You?"

Here is a IIm-V-I with an independent melody line. Try to hold the chords down for their full duration while playing the melody.

These voicings might be played in "Theme from *A Summer Place*."

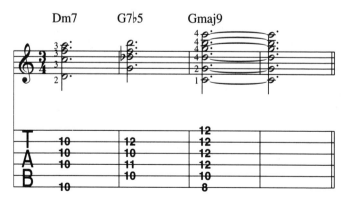

G9sus4 (G11)

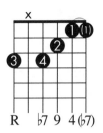

R   b7   9   4 (b7)

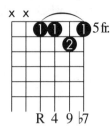

R   4   9   b7

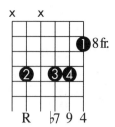

R   b7   9   4

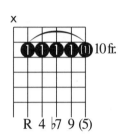

R   4   b7   9   (5)

G13

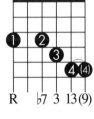

R   b7   3   13 (9)

b7   3   13   R

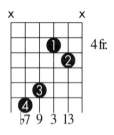

b7   9   3   13

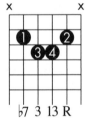

b7   3   13   R

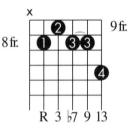

R   3   b7   9   13

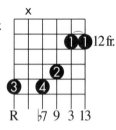

R   b7   9   3   13

G13sus4

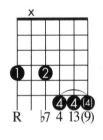

R   b7   4   13 (9)

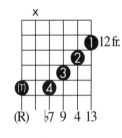

(R)   b7   9   4   13

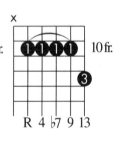

R   4   b7   9   13

b7   4   13   R

The Ninth Suspended-Fourth chord is the most popular modern substitution for the seventh chord. This example sounds like the introduction to "With a Little Luck" by Paul McCartney.

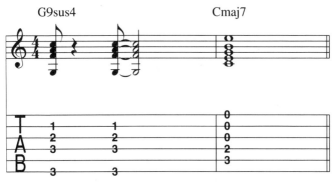

Here are the first four bars to a standard blues progression. Notice G13 is used as a substitute for G7.

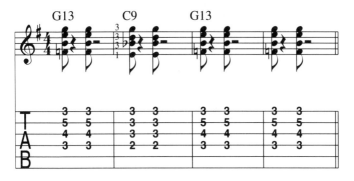

Extended chords are used to spice up this simple IIm-V-I progression and make for some smooth voice leading.

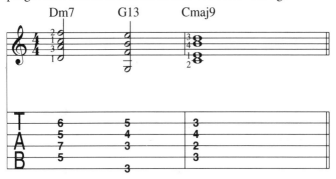

Listen to the introduction to "Manic Mechanic" by ZZ Top, and then play this funky riff. Remember that G13sus4 is just a sophisticated way of playing G7.

Augmented and Diminished Chords

G+

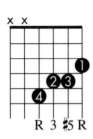

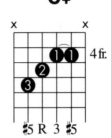

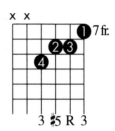

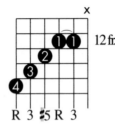

G+7 (G7♯5)

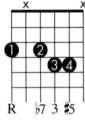

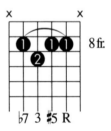

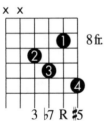

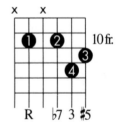

In this example, the Augmented chord is used to connect the triad with the sixth chord. You can hear this technique in Whitney Houston's "The Greatest Love of All."

The Augmented Seventh chord works beautifully as the V chord in a minor key. The E♭(D♯) is the common melody tone in this study.

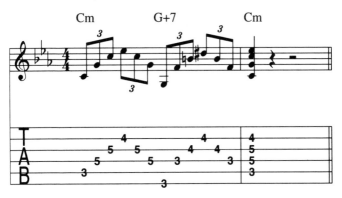

An Augmented Seventh chord can resolve to a major chord as well. Compare this exercise to the previous one.

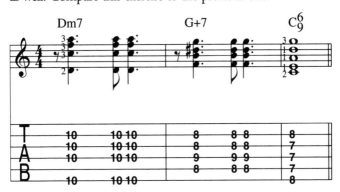

G°7

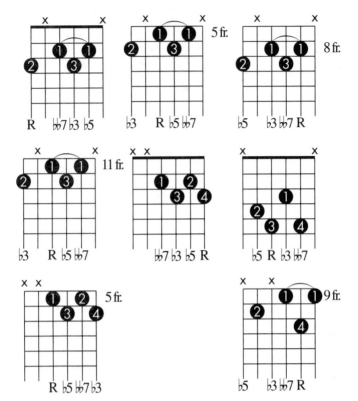

Diminished Seventh chords are made up of superimposed minor thirds. Since the interval of a minor third is equal to three frets along the guitar neck, you can move any Diminished chord form up or down three frets to produce a different inversion of the same chord. This symmetrical quality of a Diminished Seventh chord is also the reason that it may be named after any of its chord tones ($C°7=E\flat°7=G\flat°7=B\flat\flat°7$).

This example uses Diminished Seventh chords as chromatic passing chords between the I and IIm, and the IIm and IIIm chords.

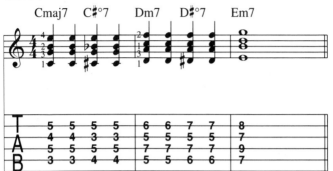

A common move in the blues is to substitute the second half of the IV chord measure with a Diminished Seventh chord a half step higher. One reason that this works so well is that the ♯IV°7 is the same as the I°7, which leads very smoothly to the I because of their common root. Play this example; you'll recognize this familiar sound.

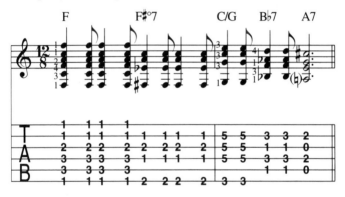

Extended and Altered Dominant Chords

G7♭9

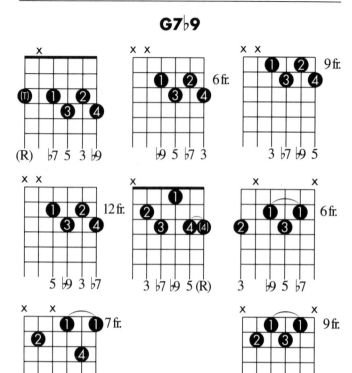

G7♯9

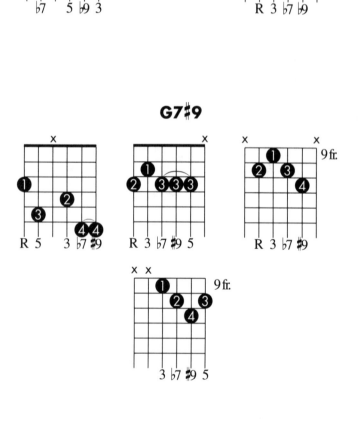

The Seventh Flat-Nine chord, like the Diminished Seventh chord, can also be moved up in minor third intervals. Here, G7♭9 smoothly resolves to Cmaj7.

The V chord may be substituted on the weak beats (2 and 4) of a static Im chord. This study is actually three bars of C Minor, but we break up the monotony by alternating the Im chord (Cm7) with the V chord (G7♭9) on every other beat.

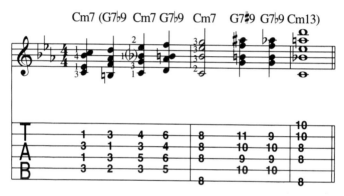

Here is a powerful introduction using the Seventh Sharp-Nine chord. Listen to "Don't Take Me Alive" by Steely Dan.

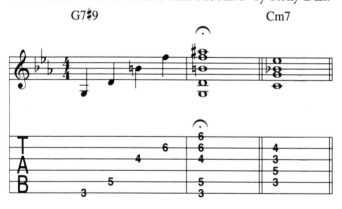

This chord is also used as a I chord. Jimi Hendrix popularized this sound in songs like "Foxy Lady."

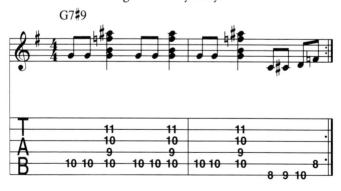

G9♯11 (G9♭5)

R 3 ♭7 9 ♯11

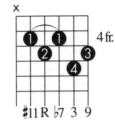

4 fr.

♯11 R ♭7 3 9

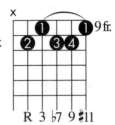

9 fr.

R 3 ♭7 9 ♯11

G+9 (G9♯5)

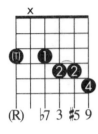

(R) ♭7 3 ♯5 9

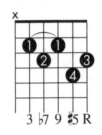

3 ♭7 9 ♯5 R

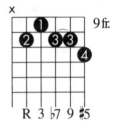

9 fr.

R 3 ♭7 9 ♯5

G13♯11 (G13♭5)

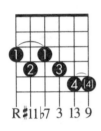

R ♯11 ♭7 3 13 9

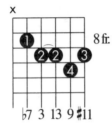

8 fr.

♭7 3 13 9 ♯11

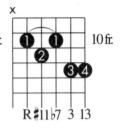

10 fr.

R ♯11 ♭7 3 13

G13♭9

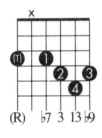

(R) ♭7 3 13 ♭9

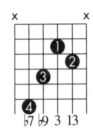

4 fr.

♭7 ♭9 3 13

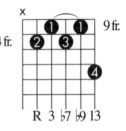

9 fr.

R 3 ♭7 ♭9 13

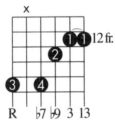

12 fr.

R ♭7 ♭9 3 13

The Ninth Sharp-Eleven chord has two uses: as a chromatic passing chord resolving down half a step, and as a substitute for the IV7 chord. In this example, the first two bars are actually a I chord (Dmaj7), but we set up the IIm chord (Em7) by substituting and playing the IV7, IIIm, and bIIIm chords over the I. This is called "backcycling." Try this concept in "Green Dolphin Street" or "The More I See You."

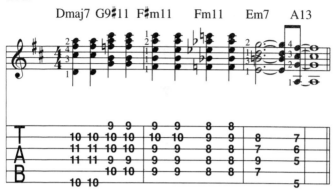

Here is a IIm-V-I using a common melody tone.

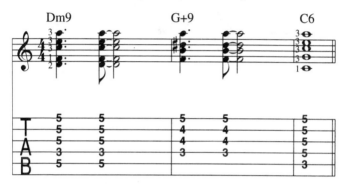

The Thirteenth Sharp-Eleven chord is an extended version of the Ninth Sharp-Eleven, so its usage is the same. Try this study in "On a Clear Day" or "What the World Needs Now."

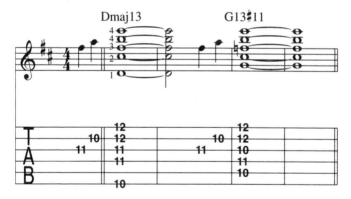

Play this IIm-V-I slowly, so you can familiarize yourself with the unique sound of the Thirteenth Flat-Nine chord.

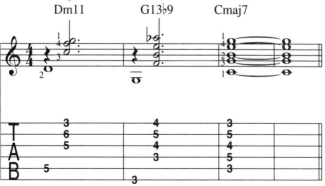

G13#9

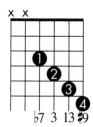

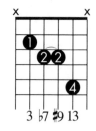

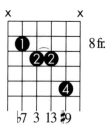

8 fr.

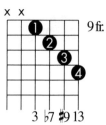

9 fr.

G7 #5 b9

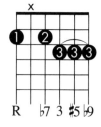

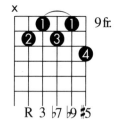

9 fr.

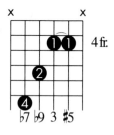

4 fr.

G7 #5 #9

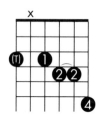

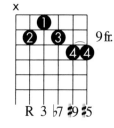

9 fr.

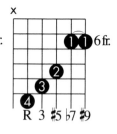

6 fr.

G7 b5 b9

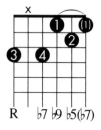

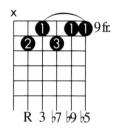

9 fr.

This is a sophisticated I-VI-II-V turnaround. It is one of jazz guitarist Tal Farlow's favorite moves.

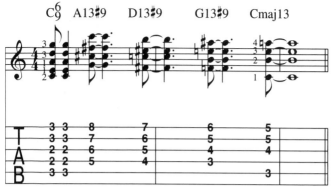

It is very important to learn different ways of playing minor, as well as major, II-V-Is. Here is a great example to study which incorporates an altered V7 chord.

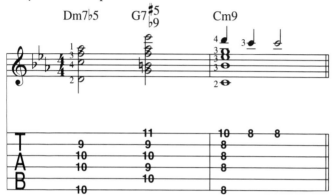

Here is a block-chord study that can be used in Duke Ellington's "Satin Doll." The voicings are what a horn section might play.

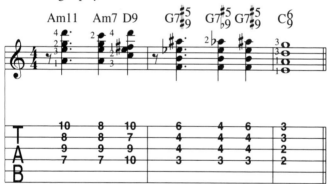

Each of the various altered dominant sounds has a distinct characteristic, and you should be able to easily distinguish one from another. This IIm-V-I will help you along.

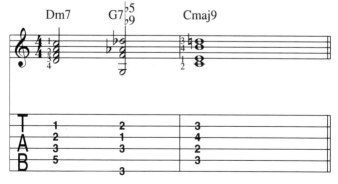

G7$\flat^5_\sharp 9$

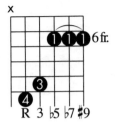

R 3 b5 b7 #9

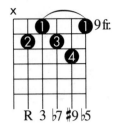

R 3 b7 #9 b5

The blues can be simple or extremely complex. This study is the first three bars of a twelve-bar blues using extended and altered dominants. Eventually you will start hearing these sounds readily.

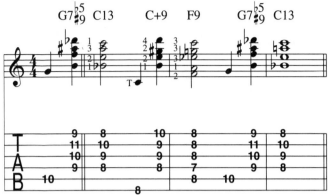

Triad Inversions

C triads

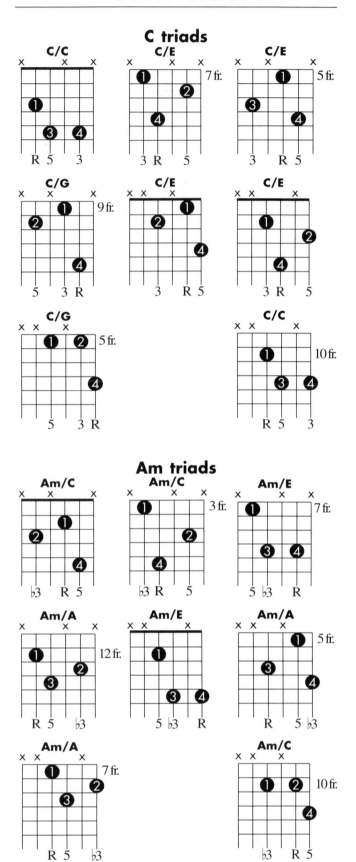

Am triads

Here is an example of voice leading. It is almost pianistic in nature. This technique is employed in classical, gospel, and even country music.

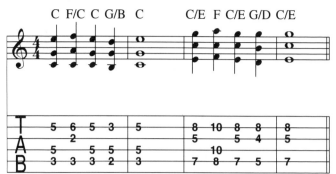

Rock guitarist Eric Johnson has incorporated this triadic approach into his improvisational style. Listen to "Cliffs of Dover," and play this study.

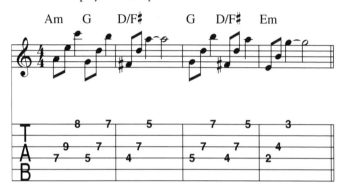

Polytonal (Slash) Chords

C/C

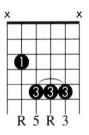

R 5 R 3

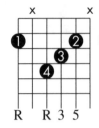

8 fr.

R R 3 5

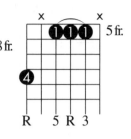

5 fr.

R 5 R 3

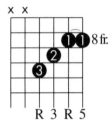

8 fr.

R 3 R 5

D♭/C (Csus4♯5♭9)

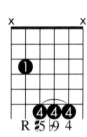

R ♯5 ♭9 4

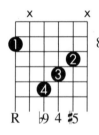

8 fr.

R ♭9 4 ♯5

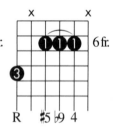

6 fr.

R ♯5 ♭9 4

D/C (C6/9♯11)

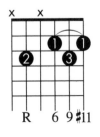

R 6 9 ♯11

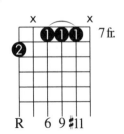

7 fr.

R 6 9 ♯11

... and they're off!

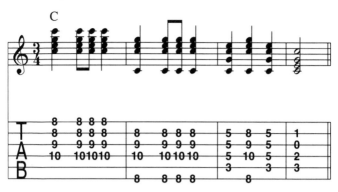

This could be a vamp in front of a Latin tune. It has a very Spanish quality.

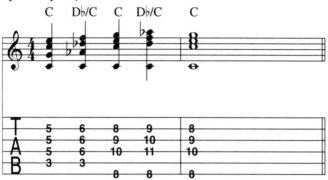

Many modern pop arrangers prefer triads with moving bass notes to traditional four- or five-voice chords, because these *slash-chord* voicings sound more "open," or hipper. Listen to this technique in "Had It All" by Whitney Houston.

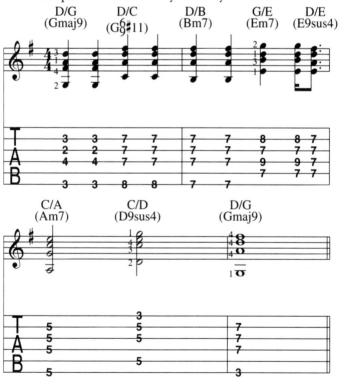

Eb/C (Cm7)

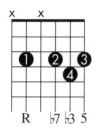

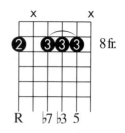

E/C (Cmaj7#5)

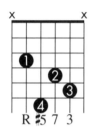

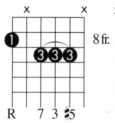

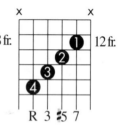

F/C (C6sus4)

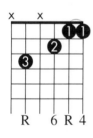

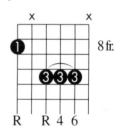

The sound of this example can be heard in the introduction to "Wishing You Were Here" by Chicago or in the verse to "Green Dolphin Street." It evokes a lot of emotion.

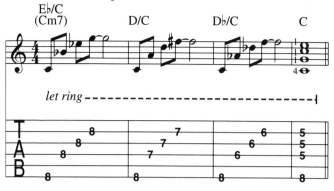

This is a very modern-sounding chord favored by innovative jazz guitarists such as John Scofield and Pat Metheny. The use of the Major Seventh Sharp-Five, rather than the more predictable Dominant Seventh Sharp-Five, can put a new spin on standards such as "Someday My Prince Will Come," "California, Here I Come," and "Of Thee I Sing."

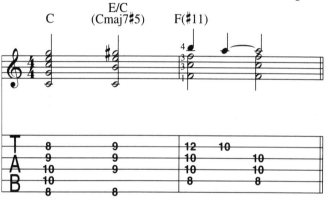

Everyone from Carole King to the Electric Light Orchestra has used this classic introduction passage. Play it, and you won't be able to "get it out of your head."

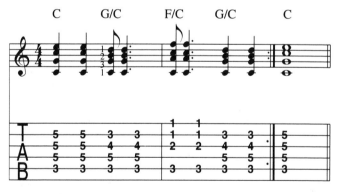

F#/C (C7♭5♭9)

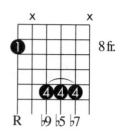

8 fr.

G/C (Cmaj9[Cmaj7sus2])

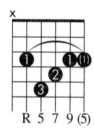

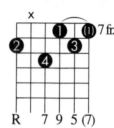

7 fr.

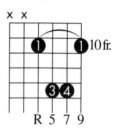

10 fr.

A♭/C (Cm#5)

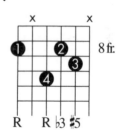

8 fr.

Here is a sophisticated way of playing a IIm-V-I. The B♭/C chord is a substitute for Gm7, while G♭/C is a substitute for C7♭5♭9. Listen to Barbra Streisand sing "Somewhere," and then play these chords.

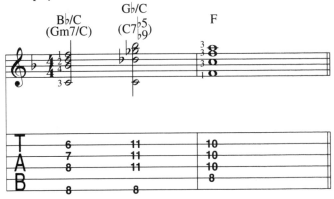

Rock supergroup Steely Dan popularized this chord. By playing the major triad a fifth above the root, you get a Major Seventh Suspended-Second. (This is usually thought of as a Major Ninth chord without the third.) This is a very modern sound, "open" and slightly different. Listen to "Deacon Blues" to hear the effect.

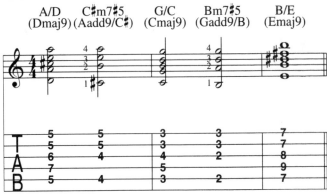

This chord is commonly used as the IIIm chord in gospel music. Listen to the tag of "Teach Me Tonight," as sung by Phoebe Snow.

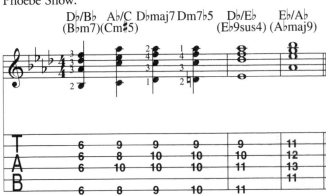

A/C (C13♭9)

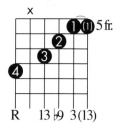

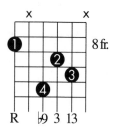

B♭/C (C9sus4)

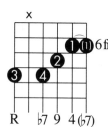

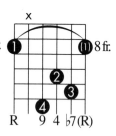

B/C (Cm[maj7] *or* Cmaj7♭5/♯9)

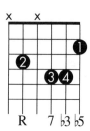

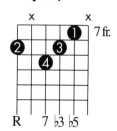

Here is another modern-sounding chord. By playing the major triad a sixth above the root, you get a Thirteenth Flat-Nine sound, but without the seventh. This example is also a reharmonized IIm-V-I study, with Bb/C (C9sus4) substituting for Gm11 and A/C substituting for C13b9. You might play this study in the first two bars of the standard "Misty."

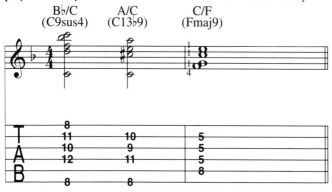

A common substitution for the Dominant Seventh chord is the Ninth Suspended-Fourth chord (C9sus4 for C7). Playing a triad a minor seventh above the root gives you that sound (Bb/C). If you listen to "You Give Good Love" by Whitney Houston, you'll hear this chord throughout the song.

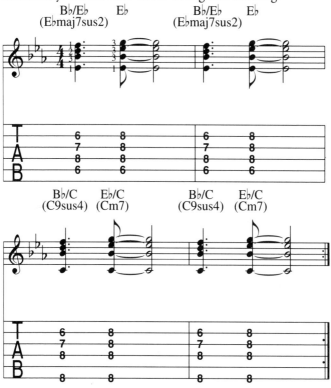

Though this chord is rarely used (except as an ending chord), it has an interesting exotic sound. You would use it as a leading chord to the tonic to give the effect of a chromatic embellishment over a stationary bass note. Try this example, which is reminiscent of the horn-section voicings of Ray Noble's closing theme, "Good Night, Sweetheart."

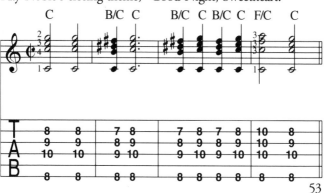

Close Voicings

Cadd9

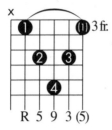
R 5 9 3 (5)

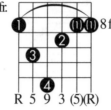
R 5 9 3 (5)(R)

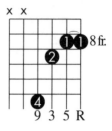
9 3 5 R

Am(add9)

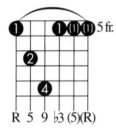
R 5 9 ♭3 (5)(R)

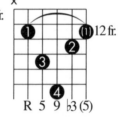
R 5 9 ♭3 (5)

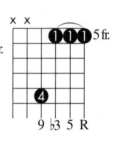
9 ♭3 5 R

Cmaj7

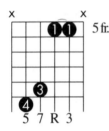
5 7 R 3

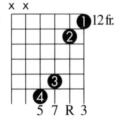
5 7 R 3

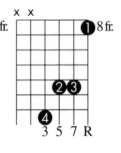
3 5 7 R

Cmaj9

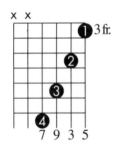
7 9 3 5

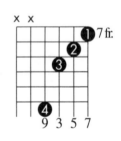
9 3 5 7

C6

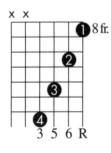
3 5 6 R

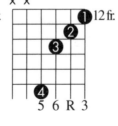
5 6 R 3

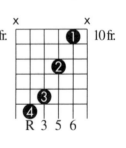
R 3 5 6

Guitarist Andy Summers of the Police frequently uses the Major Add-Nine chord. Listen to their hit "Every Breath You Take."

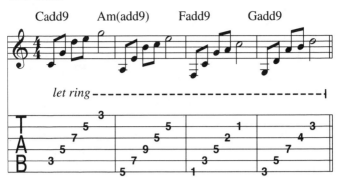

This study evokes the mood created by the theme for the television show *Twin Peaks*. Try playing this example using a lot of tremolo on your amp.

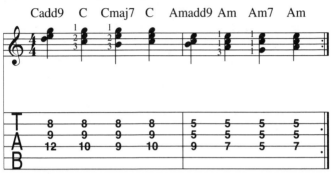

Play this voicing as a fill in songs such as "Under the Boardwalk" or "Up on the Roof" and you will mimic the sound of a pedal steel guitar. Make sure the notes ring into each other when you arpeggiate them.

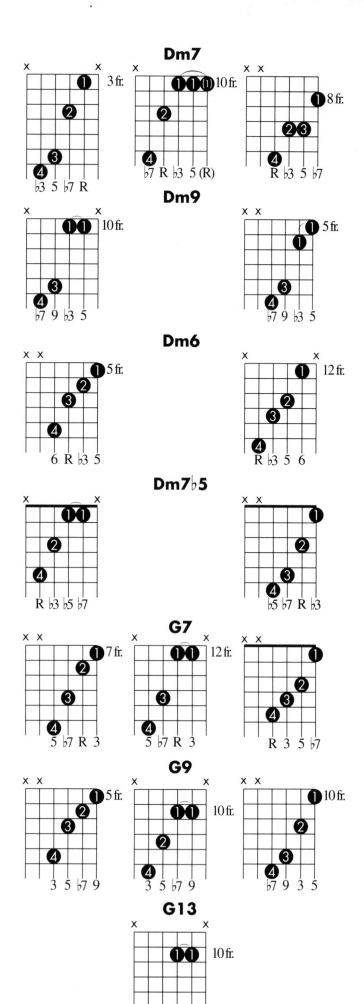

Jazz-guitar legend Johnny Smith is undoubtedly the master of the close-voiced chord. Listen to any of his recordings, especially "Moonlight in Vermont," and then try this example.

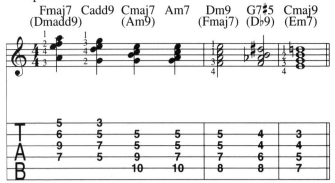

Here are two more voicings which sound like the pedal steel. They are used extensively in country and western swing music.

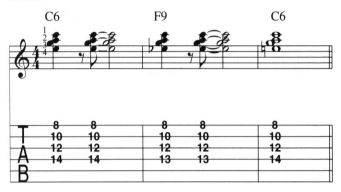

Three-Voice Chords

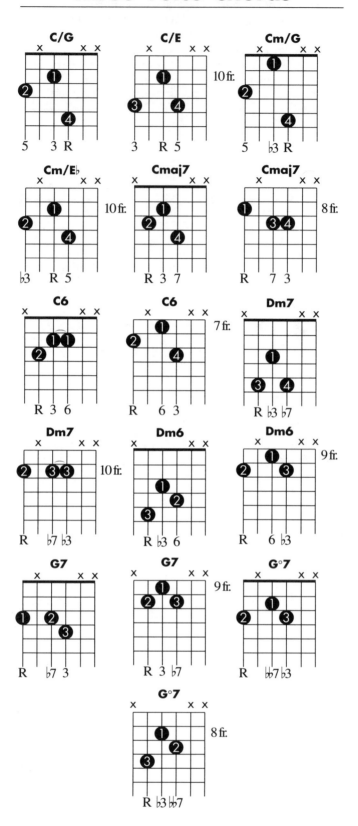

A common move in pop and jazz is to alternate between the Major Seventh and Major Sixth when comping over a static major chord. This example will remind of the introduction to "New York, New York" (as interpreted by the Chairman of the Board).

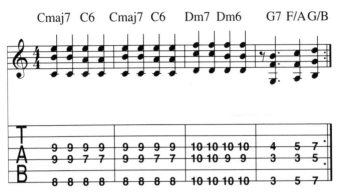

These voicings can be applied to hard rock music as well. Listen to Living Colour's "Love Rears Its Ugly Head."

This study is an example of what Freddy Green would do on a turnaround. It's a simple I-VI-II-V progression, but each chord is approached from a half step above, giving it an authentic jazz feel.

A keyboard player might approach the first two bars in a regular blues in this way; comping these voicings in the left hand while improvising a melody in the right hand. On the guitar, this approach adds a lot of interesting harmonic movement.

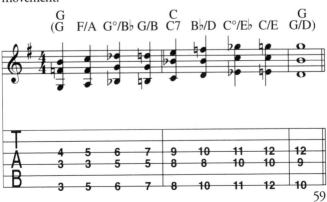

Quartal (Fourth) Voicings

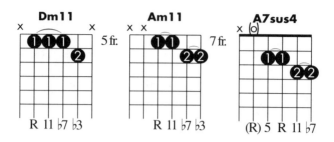

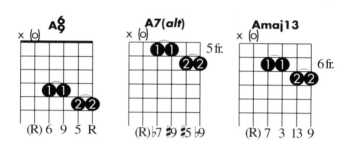

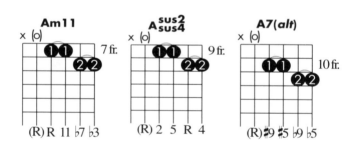

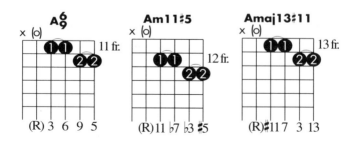

Chords built on fourths are commonly used in modern jazz and fusion music. This example sounds a lot like the classic Miles Davis tune "So What."

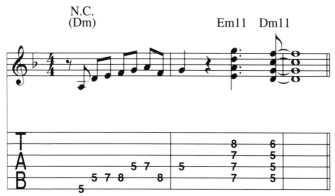

By pedaling a bass note and moving stacked fourths on top of it, you create harmonic movement not possible by playing triads. This is the foundation of modal playing. In this example, the chords imply many sounds, but the tonal center is A throughout.

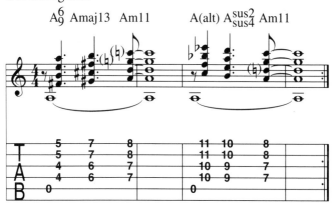

Chords with No Third

C5

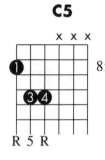
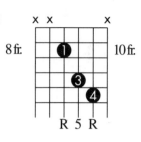

R 5 R   R 5 R   R 5 R

Csus2

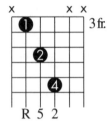
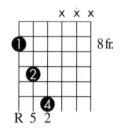

R 5 2   R 5 2

Cmaj7$^{\text{sus2}}_{\sharp 11}$

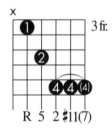
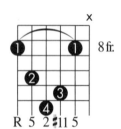

R 5 2 ♯11(7)   R 5 2 ♯11 5

C5♯11

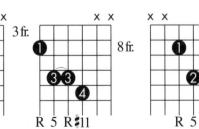
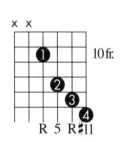

R 5 R♯11   R 5 R♯11   R 5 R♯11

This is the most widely used sound in rock and metal music. Listen to "You Really Got Me" by the Kinks or Van Halen, and crank up the distortion.

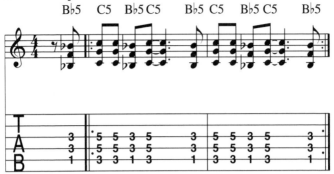

Here is another open chord that Andy Summers likes to use. Play this study after listening to "Message in a Bottle" by the Police.

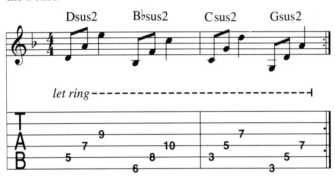

Peter Gabriel uses this haunting chord in the introduction to "Red Rain." See if you can hear this sound in the following example.

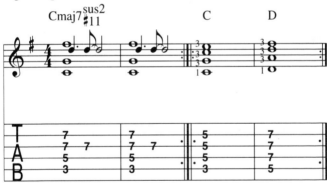

Guitar wizard Joe Satriani has a penchant for using unusual chords. Check out the introduction to "Ice 9" then take note of its similarity to this study.

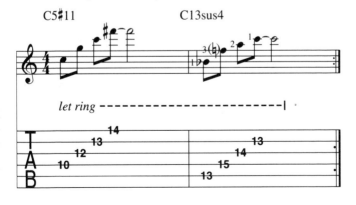

Cmaj7(no3)

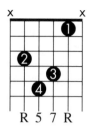

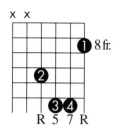

C§(no3)

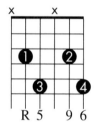

G7(no3)

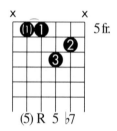

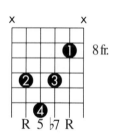

G7sus2

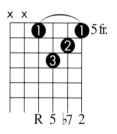

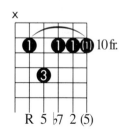

This example would make a great introduction to a contemporary pop or rhythm and blues ballad. The voicings are very pianistic. Try adding a fair amount of chorus effect when you play this one to bring out the lush quality of the chords.

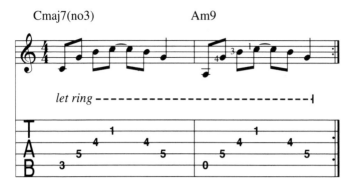

This study sounds like the soundtrack to a gladiator movie or the theme to *Outer Limits.* Notice the parallel motion of the same voicing.

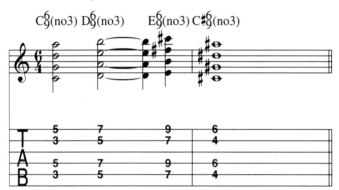

Here is a riff you might hear in the Rolling Stones' "Gimme Shelter" or Van Halen's "Top Jimmy." This is one of Keith Richard's favorite voicings.

Listen to the end of the chorus in "Fire and Rain" by James Taylor, and you'll hear this voicing. This is a popular sound in contemporary folk music.

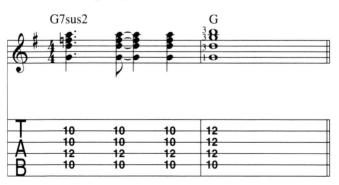

A Few Final Chords

C Major Scale Harmonized in Fourths

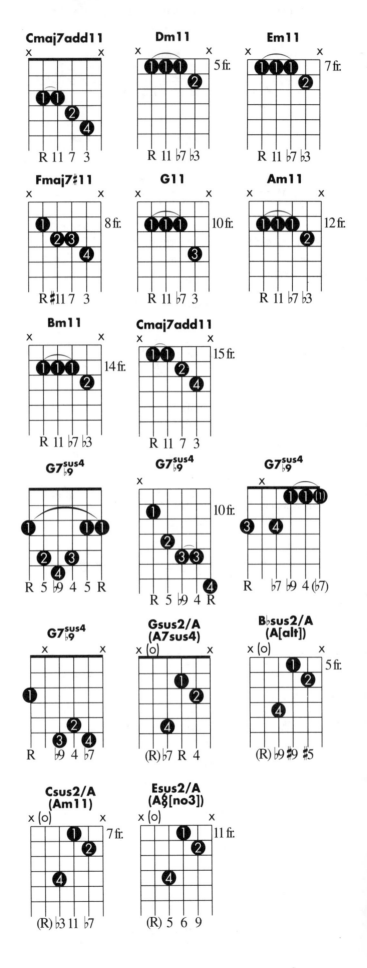

Play through this exercise to hear how different a major-scale melody can sound when harmonized in fourths. This is a technique used by many contemporary jazz players, such as John Scofield, John Abercrombie and Mick Goodrick.

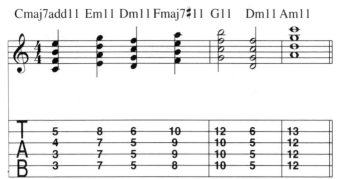

The Dominant Seventh Suspended-Fourth Flat-Nine chord has two uses: as the V chord resolving to an minor I chord, or as the tonic (I) chord in the Phrygian mode. The latter is a sound made popular by pianist Herbie Hancock. In its modal application, the chord has a Spanish flavor.

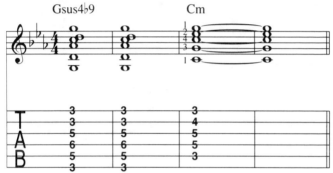

Andy Summers is one of the most innovative chord players in rock music. Here is a perfect example of controlled dissonance. Notice how seamlessly the B♭sus2/A chord flows in this progression. Listen to "Murder by Numbers" by the Police to get a better idea.

Guitar Compact Reference Books

*Here are other great titles in this series
that you will want to add to your collection:*

GUITAR

**The Advanced
Guitar Case
Chord Book**
by Askold Buk

68 pp AM 80227
ISBN 0.8256.1243.8
$4.95

Prepack AM 90176
$59.40

**The Advanced
Guitar Case
Scale Book**
by Darryl Winston

48 pp AM 91462
ISBN 0.8256.1370.1
$4.95

Prepack AM 91463
$59.40

**Basic Blues
Guitar**
by Darryl Winston

56 pp AM 91281
ISBN 0.8256.1366.3
$4.95

Prepack AM 91246
$59.40

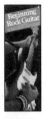

Beginning Guitar
by Artie Traum

64 pp AM 36997
ISBN 0.8256.2332.2
$4.95

Prepack AM 86997
$59.40

**Beginning Rock
Guitar**
by Artie Traum

48 pp AM 37292
ISBN 0.8256.2444.4
$4.95

Prepack AM 37300
$59.40

**The Compact
Blues Guitar
Chord Reference**
*compiled by Len
Vogler*

48 pp AM 91731
ISBN 0.8256.1385.X
$4.95

Prepack AM 91732
ISBN 0.8256.1386.8
$59.40

**The Compact
Rock Guitar
Chord Reference**
*compiled by Len
Vogler*

48pp AM 91733
ISBN 0.8256.1387.6
$4.95

Prepack AM 91734
ISBN 0.8256.1388.4
$59.40

**The Original
Guitar Case
Scale Book**
by Peter Pickow

56 pp AM 76217
ISBN 0.8256.2588.2
$4.95

Prepack AM 86217
$59.40

**Rock 'n' Roll
Guitar Case
Chord Book**
by Russ Shipton

48 pp AM 28689
ISBN 0.86001.880.6
$4.95

Prepack AM 30891
$59.40

**The Original
Guitar Case
Chord Book**
by Peter Pickow

48 pp AM 35841
ISBN 0.8256.2998.5
$4.95

Prepack AM 36138
$59.40

**Tuning Your
Guitar**
By Donald Brosnac

AM 35858
ISBN 0.8256.2180.1
$4.95

Prepack AM 85858
$59.40

BASS GUITAR

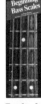

**Beginning Bass
Guitar**
by Peter Pickow

80 pp AM 36989
ISBN 0.8256.2332.4
$4.95
Prepack AM 86989
$59.40

**Beginning
Bass Scales**
by Peter Pickow

48 pp AM 87482
ISBN 0.8256.1342.6
$4.95
Prepack AM 90174
$59.40

Chord Bassics
by Jonas Hellborg

80 pp AM 60138
ISBN 0.8256.1058.3
$4.95
Prepack AM 80138
$59.40

Eight more Guitar Compact Reference Books available from Music Sales:

The Alternate Tunings Guide for Guitar
Beginning Rock Guitar
Beginning Slide Guitar
D. I. Y. Guitar Repair

Guitarist's Riff Diary
Manual de Acordes Para Guitarra
The Twelve-String Guitar Guide
Using Your Guitar

For further info contact your local music dealer or call: 1-800-431-7187